IN EVERYTHING GIVE
Thanks

LOVE GOD GREATLY MINISTRY

Contents

Welcome

WE ARE GLAD you have decided to join us in this Bible study! First of all, please know that you have been prayed for! It is not a coincidence you are participating in this study.

Our prayer for you is simple: that you will grow closer to our Lord as you dig into His Word each and every day! As you develop the discipline of being in God's Word on a daily basis, our prayer is that you will fall in love with Him even more as you spend time reading from the Bible.

Each day before you read the assigned scripture(s), pray and ask God to help you understand it. Invite Him to speak to you through His Word. Then listen. It's His job to speak to you, and it's your job to listen and obey.

Take time to read the verses over and over again. We are told in Proverbs to search and you will find: "Search for it like silver, and hunt for it like hidden treasure. Then you will understand" (Prov. 2:4–5 NCV).

We are thrilled to provide these different resources for you as you participate in our online Bible study:

- *In Everything Give Thanks* Study Journal

- Reading Plan

- Weekly Blog Posts (Mondays, Wednesdays, and Fridays)

- Weekly Memory Verses

- Weekly Monday Videos

- Weekly Challenges

- Online Community: Facebook, Twitter, Instagram, LoveGodGreatly.com

- Hashtags: #LoveGodGreatly

All of us here at Love God Greatly can't wait for you to get started, and we hope to see you at the finish line. Endure, persevere, press on—and don't give up! Finish well what you are beginning today. We will be here every step of the way, cheering you on! We are in this together. Fight to rise early, to push back the stress of the day, to sit alone and spend time in God's Word! Let's see what God has in store for you in this study! Journey with us as we learn to love God greatly with our lives!

Our Community

LOVE GOD GREATLY (LGG) is a beautiful community of women who use a variety of technology platforms to keep each other accountable in God's Word.

We start with a simple Bible reading plan, but it doesn't stop there.

Some women gather in homes and churches locally, while others connect online with women across the globe. Whatever the method, we lovingly lock arms and unite for this purpose: to love God greatly with our lives.

In today's fast-paced technology-driven world, it would be easy to study God's Word in an isolated environment that lacks encouragement or support, but that isn't the intention here at Love God Greatly. God created us to live in community with Him and with those around us.

We need each other, and we live life better together.

Because of this, would you consider reaching out and doing this study with someone?

All of us have women in our lives who need friendship, accountability, and have the desire to dive into God's Word on a deeper level. Rest assured we'll be studying right alongside you—learning with you, cheering for you, enjoying sweet fellowship, and smiling from ear to ear as we watch God unite women together—intentionally connecting hearts and minds for His glory.

It's pretty unreal, this opportunity we have to grow not only closer to God through this study but also to each other. So here's the challenge: call your mom, your sister, your grandma, the girl across the street, or the college friend across the country. Gather a group of girls from your church or workplace, or meet in a coffee shop with friends you have always wished you knew better. Utilize the beauty of connecting online for inspiration and accountability, and take opportunities to meet in person when you can.

Arm-in-arm and hand-in-hand, let's do this thing…together.

How to SOAP

WE'RE PROUD OF YOU.

We really want you to know that.

We're proud of you for making the commitment to be in God's Word, to be reading it each day and applying it to your life, the beautiful life our Lord has given you.

In this study we offer you a study journal to accompany the verses we are reading. This journal is designed to help you interact with God's Word and learn to dig deeper, encouraging you to slow down and reflect on what God is saying to you that day.

At Love God Greatly, we use the SOAP Bible study method. Before beginning, let's take a moment to define this method and share why we recommend using it during your quiet time.

Why SOAP It?

It's one thing to simply read Scripture. But when you interact with it, intentionally slowing down to really reflect on it, suddenly words start popping off the page. The SOAP method allows you to dig deeper into Scripture and see more than you would if you simply read the verses and then went on your merry way. Please take the time to SOAP through our Bible studies and see for yourself how much more you get from your daily reading. You'll be amazed.

What Does SOAP Mean?

S stands for **Scripture**. Physically write out the verses. You'll be amazed at what God will reveal to you just by taking the time to slow down and write out what you are reading!

O stands for **observation**. What do you see in the verses that you're reading? Who is the intended audience? Is there a repetition of words? What words stand out to you?

A stands for **application**. This is when God's Word becomes personal. What is God saying to you today? How can you apply what you just read to your own personal life? What changes do you need to make? Is there action you need to take?

P stands for **prayer**. Pray God's Word back to Him. Spend time thanking Him. If He has revealed something to you during this time in His Word, pray about it. If He has revealed some sin that is in your life, confess. And remember, He loves you dearly.

Follow This Example

Scripture: Read and write out Colossians 1:5–8.

> "The faith and love that spring from the hope stored up for you in heaven and about which you have already heard in the true message of the gospel that has come to you. In the same way, the gospel is bearing fruit and growing throughout the whole world— just as it has been doing among you since the day you heard it and truly understood God's grace. You learned it from Epaphras, our dear fellow servant, who is a faithful minister of Christ on our behalf, and who also told us of your love in the Spirit" (NIV).

Observation: Write what stands out to you.

> When you combine faith and love, you get hope. We must remember that our hope is in heaven; it is yet to come. The gospel is the Word of truth. The gospel is continually bearing fruit and growing from the first day to the last. It just takes one person to change a whole community…Epaphras.

Application: Apply this scripture to your own life.

> God used one man, Epaphras, to change a whole town. I was reminded that we are simply called to tell others about Christ; it's God's job to spread the gospel, to grow it, and have it bear fruit. I felt today's verses were almost directly spoken to Love God Greatly women: "The gospel is bearing fruit and growing throughout the whole world—just as it has been doing among you since the day you heard it and truly understood God's grace."

It's so fun when God's Word comes alive and encourages us in our current situation! My passionate desire is that all the women involved in our LGG Bible study will understand God's grace and have a thirst for His Word. I was moved by this quote from my Bible commentary today: "God's Word is not just for our information, it is for our transformation."

Prayer: Pray over this.

> Dear Lord, please help me to be an "Epaphras," to tell others about You and then leave the results in Your loving hands. Please help me to understand and apply personally what I have read today to my life, thereby becoming more and more like You each and every day. Help me to live a life that bears the fruit of faith and love, anchoring my hope in heaven, not here on earth. Help me to remember that the best is yet to come!

SOAP It Up

Remember, the most important ingredients in the SOAP method are your interaction with God's Word and your application of His Word to your life:

> Blessed is the one who does not walk in step with the wicked or stand in the way that sinners take or sit in the company of mockers, but whose delight is in the law of the LORD, and who meditates on his law day and night. That person is like a tree planted by streams of water, which yields its fruit in season and whose leaf does not wither—whatever they do prospers. (Ps. 1:1–3, NIV)

Reading Plan

~~~~~~~~~~

WEEK 1

Monday - GIVE THANKS
READ: Psalm 107:1-32   •   SOAP: Psalm 107:1

Tuesday - REMEMBERING & BEING THANKFUL
READ: Deuteronomy 8:1-10   •   SOAP: Deuteronomy 8:10

Wednesday - THANKING AND PROCLAIMING
READ: Isaiah 12:4-5   •   SOAP: Isaiah 12:4

Thursday - THANKSGIVING & GENEROSITY
READ: 2 Corinthians 9:6-15   •   SOAP: 2 Corinthians 9:11-12

Friday - PRAISING & HEALING
READ: Luke 17:11-19   •   SOAP: Luke 17: 17-19

Response Day

~~~~~~~~~~

WEEK 2

Monday - THANKSGIVING & PRAYER
READ: Colossians 1:3-5   •   SOAP: Colossians 1:3

Tuesday - THANKSGIVING & SONG
READ: Colossians 3:15-17   •   SOAP: Colossians 3:16-17

Wednesday - GRACE & THANKSGIVING
READ: 2 Corinthians 4:15-16   •   SOAP: 2 Corinthians 4:15

Thursday - FAITH & THANKSGIVING
READ: Colossians 2:7   •   SOAP: Colossians 2:7

Friday - THANKSGIVING IN EVERYTHING
READ: 1 Thessalonians 5:18   •   SOAP: 1 Thessalonians 5:18

Response Day

Goals

WE BELIEVE it's important to write out goals for this study. Take some time now and write three goals you would like to focus on as you begin to rise each day and dig into God's Word. Make sure and refer back to these goals throughout the next eight weeks to help you stay focused. You can do it!

My goals are:

1.

2.

3.

Signature: _____

Date: _____

Introduction

GIVE THANKS ALWAYS AND FOR EVERYTHING…

"Fleas!" I cried. "Betsie, the place is swarming with them!" We scrambled across the intervening platforms, heads low to avoid another bump, dropped down to the aisle, and edged our way to a patch of light.

"Here! And here another one!" I wailed. "Betsie, how can we live in such a place?"

"Show us. Show us how." It was said so matter of factly it took me a second to realize she was praying. More and more the distinction between prayer and the rest of life seemed to be vanishing for Betsie.

"Corrie!" she said excitedly. "He's given us the answer! Before we asked, as He always does! In the Bible this morning. Where was it? Read that part again!"

"Rejoice always, pray constantly, give thanks in all circumstances; for this is the will of God in Christ Jesus-"

"That's it, Corrie! That's His answer. 'Give thanks in all circumstances!' That's what we can do. We can start right now to thank God for every single thing about this new barracks!"

"Such as?" I said.

"Such as being assigned here together."

I bit my lip. "Oh yes, Lord Jesus!"

"Such as what you're holding in your hands."

I looked down at the Bible. "Yes! Thank You, dear Lord, that there was no inspection when we entered here! Thank You for all the women, here in this room, who will meet You in these pages."

"Yes," said Betsie. "Thank You for the very crowding here. Since we're packed so close, that many more will hear!" She looked at me expectantly. "Corrie!" she prodded.

"Oh, all right. Thank You for the jammed, crammed, stuffed packed, suffocating crowds."

"Thank You," Betsie went on serenely, "for the fleas and for-"

The fleas! This is too much. "Betsie, there's no way even God can make me grateful for a flea."

"Give thanks in all circumstances," she quoted. "It doesn't say, 'in pleasant circumstances.' Fleas are part of this place where God as put us." – *The Hiding Place, pages 209-210*

RECENTLY MY DAUGHTER, Paige, and I have been reading The Hiding Place together, and came across this story.

What a powerful reminder as we spend the next two weeks looking at the importance of being thankful in our lives.

We are reminded in Ephesians 5:20…. "always giving thanks to God the Father for everything…"

For everything, Lord?

Does God really want us to give thanks for relationships in our lives that cause us pain, for heartaches, empty bank accounts, and sick bodies? EVERYTHING?

Can we really learn to give thanks in ALL circumstances? Even for the "fleas" in our lives?

Reading Corrie's story reminds me that we can. Maybe the thanksgiving just needs, to begin with, a small prayer…

"Lord, help me to see. Open my eyes to see Your hands at work in my life."

"Help me to praise You for the 'fleas' in my life. Help me to thank You for the hard days so that I can appreciate the good ones even more."

"Thank You for giving me days when my body is weak so I'm reminded You are my strength."

"Thank You for allowing heartache and pain to enter my life so that I can experience Your sweet presence and know that You truly are near to the brokenhearted."

"Thank You, Jesus, for the forgiveness You have so graciously given to me and for opening my eyes to see my need for it."

The fleas in Corrie and Betsie's barrack were a nuisance, but God had a beautiful purpose for those pesky insects… the protection of all the women in that overcrowded barrack.

You see, the guards knew that the barrack was infested with fleas and because of that, they left the women alone. Through the fleas, God protected these women from abuse, harassment, and worse. Since the guards wanted nothing to do with those women, Corrie and Betsie were able to hold Bible studies freely without interference and women's lives were forever changed…all because of two women who choose to live their lives boldly for Christ and for God sending those tiny fleas.

And so I wonder, what "fleas" is God allowing in your life to protect you?

I'm excited to begin this two-week journey with you as we read various Scriptures daily and see what God has to say about cultivating a life of thankfulness.

Starting today, let's choose to begin seeing our lives through a lens of "gratitude" and start thanking God for EVERYTHING: the good, the bad and the "fleas" in our lives.

Love God Greatly!

-Angela

Week 1

Week 1 Challenge (Note: You can find this listed in our Monday blog post):

Prayer focus for this week: Spend time praying for your family members.

	Praying	Praise
Monday		
Tuesday		
Wednesday		
Thursday		
Friday		

Oh give thanks to the Lord,
for He is good,
for his steadfast love
endures forever!

PSALM 107:1 (ESV)

Scripture for Week 1

GIVE THANKS

MONDAY   *PSALM 107:1-32 (ESV)*

Let the Redeemed of the Lord Say So

¹ Oh give thanks to the Lord, for he is good,
   for his steadfast love endures forever!
² Let the redeemed of the Lord say so,
   whom he has redeemed from trouble
³ and gathered in from the lands,
   from the east and from the west,
   from the north and from the south.
⁴ Some wandered in desert wastes,
   finding no way to a city to dwell in;
⁵ hungry and thirsty,
   their soul fainted within them.
⁶ Then they cried to the Lord in their trouble,
   and he delivered them from their distress.
⁷ He led them by a straight way
   till they reached a city to dwell in.
⁸ Let them thank the Lord for his steadfast love,
   for his wondrous works to the children of man!
⁹ For he satisfies the longing soul,
   and the hungry soul he fills with good things.
¹⁰ Some sat in darkness and in the shadow of death,
   prisoners in affliction and in irons,
¹¹ for they had rebelled against the words of God,
   and spurned the counsel of the Most High.
¹² So he bowed their hearts down with hard labor;
   they fell down, with none to help.
¹³ Then they cried to the Lord in their trouble,
   and he delivered them from their distress.

¹⁴ He brought them out of darkness and the shadow of death,
and burst their bonds apart.
¹⁵ Let them thank the Lord for his steadfast love,
for his wondrous works to the children of man!
¹⁶ For he shatters the doors of bronze
and cuts in two the bars of iron.
¹⁷ Some were fools through their sinful ways,
and because of their iniquities suffered affliction;
¹⁸ they loathed any kind of food,
and they drew near to the gates of death.
¹⁹ Then they cried to the Lord in their trouble,
and he delivered them from their distress.
²⁰ He sent out his word and healed them,
and delivered them from their destruction.
²¹ Let them thank the Lord for his steadfast love,
for his wondrous works to the children of man!
²² And let them offer sacrifices of thanksgiving,
and tell of his deeds in songs of joy!
²³ Some went down to the sea in ships,
doing business on the great waters;
²⁴ they saw the deeds of the Lord,
his wondrous works in the deep.
²⁵ For he commanded and raised the stormy wind,
which lifted up the waves of the sea.
²⁶ They mounted up to heaven; they went down to the depths;
their courage melted away in their evil plight;
²⁷ they reeled and staggered like drunken men
and were at their wits' end.
²⁸ Then they cried to the Lord in their trouble,
and he delivered them from their distress.
²⁹ He made the storm be still,
and the waves of the sea were hushed.
³⁰ Then they were glad that the waters were quiet,
and he brought them to their desired haven.
³¹ Let them thank the Lord for his steadfast love,

for his wondrous works to the children of man!
³² Let them extol him in the congregation of the people,
and praise him in the assembly of the elders.

REMEBERING & BEING THANKFUL

TUESDAY   *DEUTERONOMY 8:1-10 (ESV)*

Remember the Lord Your God

¹ "The whole commandment that I command you today you shall be careful to do, that you may live and multiply, and go in and possess the land that the Lord swore to give to your fathers. ² And you shall remember the whole way that the Lord your God has led you these forty years in the wilderness, that he might humble you, testing you to know what was in your heart, whether you would keep his commandments or not. ³ And he humbled you and let you hunger and fed you with manna, which you did not know, nor did your fathers know, that he might make you know that man does not live by bread alone, but man lives by every word[a] that comes from the mouth of the Lord. ⁴ Your clothing did not wear out on you and your foot did not swell these forty years. ⁵ Know then in your heart that, as a man disciplines his son, the Lord your God disciplines you. ⁶ So you shall keep the commandments of the Lord your God by walking in his ways and by fearing him. ⁷ For the Lord your God is bringing you into a good land, a land of brooks of water, of fountains and springs, flowing out in the valleys and hills, ⁸ a land of wheat and barley, of vines and fig trees and pomegranates, a land of olive trees and honey, ⁹ a land in which you will eat bread without scarcity, in which you will lack nothing, a land whose stones are iron, and out of whose hills you can dig copper. ¹⁰ And you shall eat and be full, and you shall bless the Lord your God for the good land he has given you.

THANKING AND PROCLAIMING

WEDNESDAY *ISAIAH 12:4-5 (ESV)*

[4] And you will say in that day:

"Give thanks to the Lord,

call upon his name,

make known his deeds among the peoples,

proclaim that his name is exalted.

[5] "Sing praises to the Lord, for he has done gloriously;

let this be made known in all the earth.

THANKSGIVING & GENEROSITY

THURSDAY *2 CORINTHIANS 9:6-15 (ESV)*

The Cheerful Giver

[6] The point is this: whoever sows sparingly will also reap sparingly, and whoever sows bountifully will also reap bountifully. [7] Each one must give as he has decided in his heart, not reluctantly or under compulsion, for God loves a cheerful giver. [8] And God is able to make all grace abound to you, so that having all sufficiency in all things at all times, you may abound in every good work. [9] As it is written,

"He has distributed freely, he has given to the poor;
his righteousness endures forever."

[10] He who supplies seed to the sower and bread for food will supply and multiply your seed for sowing and increase the harvest of your righteousness. [11] You will be enriched in every way to be generous in every way, which through us will produce thanksgiving to God. [12] For the ministry of this service is not only supplying the needs of the saints but is also overflowing in many thanksgivings

to God. [13] By their approval of this service, they will glorify God because of your submission that comes from your confession of the gospel of Christ, and the generosity of your contribution for them and for all others, [14] while they long for you and pray for you, because of the surpassing grace of God upon you.[15] Thanks be to God for his inexpressible gift!

PRAISING & HEALING

FRIDAY   *LUKE 17:11-19 (ESV)*

[11] On the way to Jerusalem he was passing along between Samaria and Galilee. [12] And as he entered a village, he was met by ten lepers,[a] who stood at a distance [13] and lifted up their voices, saying, "Jesus, Master, have mercy on us." [14] When he saw them he said to them, "Go and show yourselves to the priests." And as they went they were cleansed.[15] Then one of them, when he saw that he was healed, turned back, praising God with a loud voice; [16] and he fell on his face at Jesus' feet, giving him thanks. Now he was a Samaritan. [17] Then Jesus answered, "Were not ten cleansed? Where are the nine? [18] Was no one found to return and give praise to God except this foreigner?" [19] And he said to him, "Rise and go your way; your faith has made you well."

Monday

READ: Psalm 107:1-32

SOAP: Psalm 107:1

Scripture - Write out the **Scripture** passage for the day.

Observations - Write down 1 or 2 **observations** from the passage.

Monday

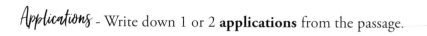

Applications - Write down 1 or 2 **applications** from the passage.

Pray - Write out a **prayer** over what you learned from today's passage.

-Visit our website today for the corresponding blog post!-

Tuesday

READ: Deuteronomy 8:1-10

SOAP: Deuteronomy 8:10

Scripture - Write out the **Scripture** passage for the day.

Observations - Write down 1 or 2 **observations** from the passage.

Tuesday

Applications - Write down 1 or 2 **applications** from the passage.

Pray - Write out a **prayer** over what you learned from today's passage.

Wednesday

READ: Isaiah 12:4-5
SOAP: Isaiah 12:4

Scripture - Write out the **Scripture** passage for the day.

Observations - Write down 1 or 2 **observations** from the passage.

Wednesday

Applications - Write down 1 or 2 **applications** from the passage.

Pray - Write out a **prayer** over what you learned from today's passage.

-Visit our website today for the corresponding blog post!-

Thursday

READ: 2 Corinthians 9:6-15
SOAP: 2 Corinthians 9:11-12

Scripture - Write out the **Scripture** passage for the day.

Observations - Write down 1 or 2 **observations** from the passage.

Thursday

Applications - Write down 1 or 2 **applications** from the passage.

Pray - Write out a **prayer** over what you learned from today's passage.

READ: Luke 17:11-19
SOAP: Luke 17: 17-19

Scripture - Write out the **Scripture** passage for the day.

Observations - Write down 1 or 2 **observations** from the passage.

Friday

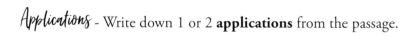

Applications - Write down 1 or 2 **applications** from the passage.

Pray - Write out a **prayer** over what you learned from today's passage.

-Visit our website today for the corresponding blog post!-

Reflection Questions

1. What are some ways God has been good to you in your life? List a few and take the time today to thank Him.

2. It is important to look back on your life and remember God's faithfulness. How has God showed His faithfulness to you over the years?

3. We shouldn't keep our gratitude for God to ourselves; we need to proclaim it to those in our lives. What is one way you can start proclaiming God's faithfulness in your life starting today?

4. Why is it important for Christians to be generous? What impact would it have on the world if Christians no longer were generous with the resources God has given to them? Looking at your life, are there ways you can be more generous with your time, resources or finances?

5. Jesus healed all ten lepers, but only one came back to thank Him. What are some ways you can guard your heart against ungratefulness?

My Response

Week 2

Week 2 Challenge (Note: You can find this listed in our Monday blog post):

Prayer focus for this week: Spend time praying for your country.

	Praying	Praise
Monday		
Tuesday		
Wednesday		
Thursday		
Friday		

Give thanks in all circumstances;
for this is the will of God
in Christ Jesus for you.

1 THESSALONIANS 5:18 (ESV)

Scripture for Week 2

THANKSGIVING & PRAYER

MONDAY   *COLOSSIANS 1:3-5 (ESV)*

[3] We always thank God, the Father of our Lord Jesus Christ, when we pray for you, [4] since we heard of your faith in Christ Jesus and of the love that you have for all the saints,[5] because of the hope laid up for you in heaven. Of this you have heard before in the word of the truth, the gospel,

---

THANKSGIVING & SONG

TUESDAY   *COLOSSIANS 3:15-17 (ESV)*

[15] And let the peace of Christ rule in your hearts, to which indeed you were called in one body. And be thankful. [16] Let the word of Christ dwell in you richly, teaching and admonishing one another in all wisdom, singing psalms and hymns and spiritual songs, with thankfulness in your hearts to God. [17] And whatever you do, in word or deed, do everything in the name of the Lord Jesus, giving thanks to God the Father through him.

GRACE & THANKSGIVING

WEDNESDAY   *2 CORINTHIANS 4:15-16 (ESV)*

[15] For it is all for your sake, so that as grace extends to more and more people it may increase thanksgiving, to the glory of God.

[16] So we do not lose heart. Though our outer self is wasting away, our inner self is being renewed day by day.

FAITH & THANKSGIVING

THURSDAY   *COLOSSIANS 2:7 (ESV)*

[7] rooted and built up in him and established in the faith, just as you were taught, abounding in thanksgiving.

THANKSGIVING IN EVERYTHING

FRIDAY   *1 THESSALONIANS 5:18 (ESV)*

[18] give thanks in all circumstances; for this is the will of God in Christ Jesus for you.

Monday

READ: Colossians 1:3-5

SOAP: Colossians 1:3

Scripture - Write out the **Scripture** passage for the day.

Observations - Write down 1 or 2 **observations** from the passage.

Monday

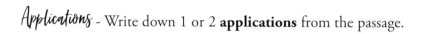

Applications - Write down 1 or 2 **applications** from the passage.

Pray - Write out a **prayer** over what you learned from today's passage.

-Visit our website today for the corresponding blog post!-

Tuesday

READ: Colossians 3:15-17
SOAP: Colossians 3:16-17

Scripture - Write out the **Scripture** passage for the day.

Observations - Write down 1 or 2 **observations** from the passage.

Tuesday

Applications - Write down 1 or 2 **applications** from the passage.

Pray - Write out a **prayer** over what you learned from today's passage.

Wednesday

READ: 2 Corinthians 4:15-16

SOAP: 2 Corinthians 4:15

Scripture - Write out the **Scripture** passage for the day.

Observations - Write down 1 or 2 **observations** from the passage.

Wednesday

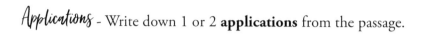

Applications - Write down 1 or 2 **applications** from the passage.

Pray - Write out a **prayer** over what you learned from today's passage.

-Visit our website today for the corresponding blog post!-

Thursday

READ: Colossians 2:7
SOAP: Colossians 2:7

Scripture - Write out the **Scripture** passage for the day.

Observations - Write down 1 or 2 **observations** from the passage.

Thursday

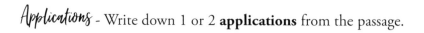

Applications - Write down 1 or 2 **applications** from the passage.

Pray - Write out a **prayer** over what you learned from today's passage.

Friday

READ: 1 Thessalonians 5:18
SOAP: 1 Thessalonians 5:18

Scripture - Write out the **Scripture** passage for the day.

Observations - Write down 1 or 2 **observations** from the passage.

Friday

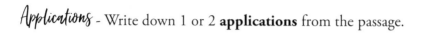

Applications - Write down 1 or 2 **applications** from the passage.

Pray - Write out a **prayer** over what you learned from today's passage.

-Visit our website today for the corresponding blog post!-

Reflection Questions

1. It is important to acknowledge our thankfulness, especially for those God has placed in our lives. A wonderful way to show your gratitude is by praying and thanking God for those in your life! Who are you most thankful for today and why? Take time today to thank God for this special friend.

2. What are some ways you can start cultivating more thankfulness in your heart?

3. I've seen it in my life, the more someone has needed God's amazing grace, the more they seem to live lives characterized with thankfulness. Why do you think the two are so closely connected?

4. We are called to give thanks to God in all circumstances of our lives, yet this can be so hard to do when we are hurting, disappointed or discouraged. Take time today to ask God to open your eyes so that you can see His hand at work in your life and choose to be thankful.

5. Now that you've been focusing on gratitude in your life these last two weeks, what are some changes you are going to make to cultivate a life of thanksgiving?

My Response

How Can You Know That You Are Forgiven?

Know these truths from God's Word...

God loves you.

Even when you're feeling unworthy and like the world is stacked against you, God loves you - *yes, you* - and He has created you for great purpose.

> God's Word says, "God so loved the world that He gave His one and only Son, Jesus, that whoever believes in Him shall not perish, but have eternal life" (John 3:16).

Our sin separates us from God.

We are all sinners by nature and by choice, and because of this we are separated from God, who is holy.

> God's Word says, "All have sinned and fall short of the glory of God" (Romans 3:23).

Jesus died so that you might have life.

The consequence of sin is death, but your story doesn't have to end there! God's free gift of salvation is available to us because Jesus took the penalty for our sin when He died on the cross.

God's Word says, "For the wages of sin is death, but the free gift of God is eternal life in Christ Jesus our Lord" (Romans 6:23); "God demonstrates His own love toward us, in that while we were yet sinners, Christ died for us" (Romans 5:8).

Jesus lives!

Death could not hold Him, and three days after His body was placed in the tomb Jesus rose again, defeating sin and death forever! He lives today in heaven and is preparing a place in eternity for all who believe in Him.

God's Word says, "In my Father's house are many rooms. If it were not so, would I have told you that I go to prepare a place for you? And if I go and prepare a place for you, I will come again and will take you to myself, that where I am you may be also" (John 14:2-3).

Yes, you can KNOW that you are forgiven.

Accept Jesus as the only way to salvation…

Accepting Jesus as your Savior is not about what you can do, but rather about having faith in what Jesus has already done. It takes recognizing that you are a sinner, believing that Jesus died for your sins, and asking for forgiveness by placing your full trust in Jesus's work on the cross on your behalf.

God's Word says, "If you confess with your mouth that Jesus is Lord and believe in your heart that God raised him from the dead, you will be saved. For with the heart one believes and is justified, and with the mouth one confesses and is saved" (Romans 10:9-10).

Practically, what does that look like? With a sincere heart, you can pray a simple prayer like this:

God,

I know that I am a sinner.

I don't want to live another day without embracing

the love and forgiveness that You have for me.

I ask for Your forgiveness.

I believe that You died for my sins and rose from the dead.

I surrender all that I am and ask You to be Lord of my life.

Help me to turn from my sin and follow You.

Teach me what it means to walk in freedom as I live under Your grace,

and help me to grow in Your ways as I seek to know You more.

Amen.

If you just prayed this prayer (or something similar in your own words), would you email us at info@lovegodgreatly.com? We'd love to help get you started on this exciting journey as a child of God!

a LoveGodGreatly Bible Study Journal

David

HIS STORY IS OUR STORY

Welcome, friend. We're so glad you're here...

LOVE GOD GREATLY exists to inspire, encourage, and equip women all over the world to make God's Word a priority in their lives.

-INSPIRE-

women to make God's Word a priority in their daily lives through our Bible study resources.

-ENCOURAGE-

women in their daily walks with God through online community and personal accountability.

-EQUIP-

women to grow in their faith, so that they can effectively reach others for Christ.

Love God Greatly consists of a beautiful community of women who use a variety of technology platforms to keep each other accountable in God's Word.

We start with a simple Bible reading plan, but it doesn't stop there.

Some gather in homes and churches locally, while others connect online with women across the globe. Whatever the method, we lovingly lock arms and unite for this purpose...

to Love God Greatly with our lives.

At *Love God Greatly*, you'll find real, authentic women. Women who are imperfect, yet forgiven. Women who desire less of us, and a whole lot more of Jesus. Women who long to know God through his Word, because we know that Truth transforms and sets us free. **Women who are better together, saturated in God's Word and in community with one another.**

Love God Greatly is a 501 (C) (3) non-profit organization. Funding for Love God Greatly comes through donations and proceeds from our online Bible study journals and books. LGG is committed to providing quality Bible study materials and believes finances should never get in the way of a woman being able to participate in one of our studies. All LGG journals and translated journals are available to downloaded for free from LoveGodGreatly.com for those who cannot afford to purchase them. Our journals and books are also available for sale on Amazon. Search for "Love God Greatly" so see all our Bible study journals and books. 100% of proceeds go directly back into supporting Love God Greatly and helping us inspire, encourage and equip women all over the world with God's Word.

THANK YOU for partnering with us!

What we offer:

18 + Translations | Bible Reading Plans | Online Bible Study
Love God Greatly App | 80 + Countries Served
Bible Study Journals & Books | Community Groups

Each Love God Greatly study includes:

Three Devotional Coorsesponding Blog Posts | Monday Vlog Videos
Memory Verses | Weekly Challenge | Weekly Reading Plan
Reflection Questions And More!

Other Love God Greatly studies include:

David | Ecclesiastes | Growing Through Prayer | Names Of God
Galatians | Psalm 119 | 1St & 2Nd Peter | Made For Community | Esther
The Road To Christmas | The Source Of Gratitude | You Are Loved

36494277R00035

Made in the USA
Middletown, DE
03 November 2016